A LONG DARK SUMMER

poems

Helenna Santos

A Long Dark Summer
Copyright © 2021 by Helenna Santos.

All rights reserved.
Inquiries should be addressed to
helenna@mightypharaohfilms.com

Cover design by Helenna Santos
Cover layout by Dog & Pony Creative
Formatting by Polgarus Studio

ISBN: 978-0-9908822-2-0 (trade paperback)
ISBN: 978-0-9908822-3-7 (kindle)
ISBN: 978-0-9908822-4-4 (epub)

First edition: June 2021

For
my Grandfather, Walter Muralt,
who I never met but have always known.

Contents

Las Vegas Snow Globe 1

1993 3
    Thanks a lot '90s 5
    lower case 8
    twins 9
    Teen Hotline 11
    Cult 12
    creation 13
    Mixed Tape Maniac 14

2002 15
    Musician Man 17
    Poetess 19
    Bird House 20
    Nights with Leonard 21
    Wake. 23
    Mistress Ophelia 24
    War Paint 26
    That One Summer 27

2005 29
    Los Angeles 31
    Take Out 33
    Neo-politan 35
    Down Town 36

- Terminated 38
- construction 39

2007 41
- Cocktail Waitress 43
- Just one more? 44
- Fine Dining Fight Club 45
- Penny Lane 46
- the housewife in apartment 12B 48

2013 49
- The Assassination 51
- the expedition 52
- For Cindy: My Blue Valentine 53
- This Will Be Televised 55
- inside these moving pictures 56
- Paul-y Pocket 58
- Social-ism 59
- 140 Characters 60

2016 61
- Road Trip Renegade 63
- Captive 65
- Natural Selection 66
- Sadie and the Salton Sea 68

2020 71
- Writer's Block 73
- Happily 74

   a long dark summer.. 76
   punctuate.. 78

2021.. 79
   All the world's a stage. 81

Acknowledgements... 83
About the Author 85

"Don't count yourself out this early, Daisy. You're all sorts of things you don't even know yet."

–Taylor Jenkins Reid,
Daisy Jones and the Six

A LONG
DARK SUMMER

Las Vegas Snow Globe

You shake me and I fly
above the clouds
in this curved round world.

Light reflecting on the covered glass desert.

Flying
blind above the sky
knees scraping
along the Care Bear clouds of
silver and gold flecked stars and hearts
weightless
wandering
floating
falling
grasping onto the plastic hands of Elvis.

We all go down eventually.

Hitting land
tumbling
and
running
arms outstretched
grasping
at the beautiful steam of this mirage.

I know this place,
what it wants from me
organized chaos
and
repetition
in a single instant
it scares me still
we are always moving
organs pumping
breath quivering.

I'll forever be afraid of this giant curved womb.

I flounder
among these hotels
and casinos
and giant palm trees,
until you shake me again.
uproot me.

And organized chaos begins once more.

Me, your miniature Las Vegas showgirl
in plastic sequin
plastic queen in
your perfect
plastic world.

1993

Thanks a lot '90s

I've always been a sucker for a road trip movie.

Correction.

A "girl on a road trip" movie.

Drew Barrymore. *Mad Love*.

That movie's soundtrack on constant repeat
dancing around and around and around
my room before going to school every day
when I was fifteen years old.

It made all of the anxious energy I felt inside me,
all of the crazy,
exceptionally normal.

No. Not normal.
Not. Normal.
Special.

I was special.

I was the only one who knew exactly
what Drew Barrymore's character was feeling
when she swam all the way across

that freezing cold vast whole huge dark scary lake
in the middle of the night to see Chris O'Donnell.

Drew and I.
We understood one another.

We overplucked our eyebrows
wore army boots with lingerie dresses overtop of white t-shirts
we drove VW bugs
and cut out photos from teen magazines
and stuck those pictures all over our white barren walls.

And I wished.
I wished
and wished
and wished

and wanted to have enough guts to cut all of my hair off
and have tiny bangs that barely covered half of my forehead.

And
I wished.

I wished to be white.

I wished I was blonde
and skinny
and white.

But my half-Filipino body barred any of that
from being a real dream to strive for
and it was just a fantasy just
like I knew that movie road trip journey
was never going to last
that Drew and Chris
would have to go home soon
and return back to the reality that they came from.

But that freedom.

That freedom I felt watching her
stand up in that jeep driving down that winding road
hair all short and cute and sexy
all blowing in the wind as Chris drove her into the sunset?

I watched that over and over and over and over
rewinding the VHS until the tape was mostly all static.

That freedom.
That. Freedom.

That freedom of Drew's.

That's a freedom I've been trying to find ever since.

lower case

i'm writing everything in lower case like e.e. cummings so that means it's artistic and important and I'll make an impact on the world right?

twins

half of me and half of you
conjoined.

seeing us together confuses the townspeople.

parasitic twins we walk carrying two lives
on one body's limbs
sharing pleasure, pain, and joy.

your tastes are your own as are mine.

vanilla ice cream versus rocky road
in crunchy waffle cones on a hot August evening.

although we share this heart
this bleeding, feeling heart
that lusts and longs for the boy next door.

i tried to sever us once from each other
took Mama's kitchen knife from the yellow drawer
but all I could do was sit there weeping on
the cold linoleum floor.

formica table above my head
and your eyes staring at me
not a tear in sight

and all we could feel was the pounding of our heart,
the heaving of our chest
and the knowledge that this
is
beautifully, sadly, and terribly
forever.

Teen Hotline

This skin isn't fair. It isn't my own.

It lies to me
hides me.

I slice into it with thoughts
and words
and try to burn it away
with a sip of whiskey from
my Dad's wooden liquor cabinet.

But all it took was one call
to the 1-800 teen hotline
from our white rotary phone…

to understand

Asian + alcohol = red.

Cult

We are exactly where we are supposed to be
In this kaleidoscope of discovery
A childhood observatory
Only seen from on our knees.
A coat of many colors
Ezekiel and the wheel
And we're expected to kneel
Hands in the air
Into your lair
A real legion
Of this religion
So that we can recruit
For this violent assembly
Abhorrent normality
In a twisted morality
Denying all reality

creation

I was not born of your side
in the midst of some hollow day
by the hand of a man
who needed a scapegoat for his sins.

I emerged quite holy
on my own
yet allowing you to claim me
to carry on with the fable.

Mixed Tape Maniac

a story of a life

in unfinished b-sides

melodies and harmonies and dissonance
ballads and up-tempo

never all one style but
all could be played
'round midnight
with a whiskey
or a wine
or a cherry coke

spoken word
operatic screams

jazz jazz jazz
live sounds and screeching owls
inner city growls

as Lisa Loeb begs, Stay
while Alanis tells you it's ironic
that Jewel asks who will save your soul

all before we flip to side B

2002

Musician Man

A restless, restless evening
of way too much weed and Nirvana
On the CD player spinning.
Waiting for him to come home.

My body has become a lost and found.
A playground for pains.

It's all about these Rock Stars.
Like living candy bars
Like jelly, all over me
So that everyone can see how his gaze transfixes me.

Kisses, Kisses
Wish I was his Mrs.
All the while my head is spinning as I
grow closer to the end of this flat, paved world.

And there he goes again.
Onto the Road with scholars doing magic tricks,
Just like in the flicks.
Fake flickering wicks of his ecstasy.

And I believed it all.

While he was having sex with me
Like bitter Blasphemy,

My gouging glittering golden God.

Poetess

I speak in fragments.
In stilted parables.

You may not understand me.
You may not care to try.

But I am both deaf and dumb.
To your audible sighs.

Because I propose.
There is no purpose.
To anything in excess.
In this world's catastrophic mess.

So, I minimize.
And I fantasize.
That in each of us lies.
What is wholly wise.
And doesn't need full sentences.
To run on.
And on.
And on with.

Bird House

House me inside you
a small refugee.

Through flesh and muscle
bone and breath
I hide myself
in order to fold into a piece of you.

Leave me silent.
Let me be.
Do not even ask me to breathe.

For if I do
if I did
I would find myself
in the very act of aspiring to flee
this safe haven
of you.

Nights with Leonard

There were those times
when Leonard Cohen and I
would sit together
on a Sunday evening by the fire
and swoon to each other
over a glass of shiraz.

He would speak to me in flickering words
About sex
And coffee
And you.

He spoke of the lovers
in the house
knowing only of each other.

Now I (a voyeur to this old encounter)
begin to cry.

It's no longer him speaking to me.

It's you.
Under the covers

Late at night
in our bed

QUICKLY

before the light comes up
before the alarm goes off
before the cat bites at your toes
and runs circles 'round your head.

You take me there
to Cohen's room,
to his lovers,
to his lips.

And kissing you
feels just as sweet
as seeing the shining sweat
on your ivory skin.

Until the wine is sipped,
Each
Drop
Dry

Each

Novella.

Wake.

Lie-ing there
the sun rises over your shoulder
cutting us into mourning

murdered sharp shards
left over on my bedroom floor
from our paper doll hands fused
forever tragically stuck
together.

Mistress Ophelia

Why is this so goddam sexy?
Captivating.
Hovering on water.
Still life flying on wet wispy clouds downriver.

Wailing herons and dancing gulls ring around my mind in flocks
and in too-bright sunshine, too-dark moonlight
taking flight like a dove
fluttering.

I, there's the rub.

Soaking my body.
In this space between
dreaming of that mountain stream
away, away, floating away.

Until
I turn the tap off.

Quiet
Like I never knew this bathroom.
That it's so incredibly bright and hollow and dark.

And
I let out the water.
Let out the wander.
Let out the wonder.

Until the next time I decide I'm unclean.

War Paint

I knew you would leave like this.

As T.S. Eliot says, "not with a bang but a whimper."

You were already out the door
and I didn't know I was weaponized for war.

Brushes and paints and glue
an attempted gift for you
from the specialty craft store
open
9 to 5
on the corner.

And in my hands is a reading rainbow
that I'll hide in my art kit
in my basement below.

Because all I have left
is this cold blank slate
an oversized canvas
void of any color.

That One Summer

I put you in the frame
I bought from Amazon for $2.99.
Didn't know what else to do with you.

Didn't know how to let go
of that 2002 motorcycle trip to Tofino
in the pouring rain.

It's a shit photo.

Your leather jacket
the only thing in focus
walking away from me
the way you always did.

Romanticizing the mundane
in the idiocy
of a stupid girl
in love.

All I brought was a toothbrush and a wallet
for an entire weekend trip
in an act of indignant defiance.

You.

Drummer number 4.

You were the first and the last,
best stupid decision I ever made.

Except maybe for this.
This $2.99 spent on a picture frame.

The cost to hang on to lost love
and memory lane.

2005

Los Angeles

The fries from McDonald's are utterly disappointing.
Stepping away from my no-carb rule has been a bust.

Sitting here at LAX I am at a crossroads.
Los Angeles is no longer what I see on "Entourage"

Glitz, Glamour, Sun, Surf,
Big Boobs, Small Dogs, Fast Cars, Fast Women.
Grey Goose, Angels, and Champagne

It's the place that I learned that none of this,
none of it, is real.

Where Grey Goose Flows Like Water.

A red head's dark shadow.
Please let me be white and blonde, tall and important.

Tears tearing up my insides,
Waiting for the plane
To take me.

Strange heels, sunglasses, necklaces so perfect.
Perfect. Perfect. People.

Can't move. Can't speak.
What incredible fun.

God, just get me home.

Take Out

I was served to you in a single serving wrapper.
Litter, trash, unrecyclable.

Pre-spiced, half baked
it made it easy
for you to throw me in
on the highest setting for two minutes
too long
but you ignored the instructions
because I came in perfectly marketed packaging.

Bought with a coupon
sent to you by a friend
sent by their friend
and the friend, of a friend, of a friend.

A perverted potluck.

Finger-licking, spitting
narrowly resisting
as that metal knife cuts in deep.

And here you are
throwing out half
as if
tasteless, baseless, and vile.

Gluttony
misogyny
custom curated
for world-wide
cultural mass consumption.

Neo-politan

if this is all just The Matrix

if there is no spoon

how do I eat this fucking fro-yo?

Down Town

What is there to learn from the everyday
from the grind?

Walking blindly beside each other
not smelling the desperate hopeless stench
of the businessman on the corner
waiting for green
for Go.

Mothers
Strippers
Lovers
Killers
Everyone trying to get by.

Walk, don't walk.
Caught in a perpetual yellow light.

In Traffic,
needing to be somewhere by 3pm.
Now.
Late.

Sisyphus on the mountain.

Where does all of the time go?

Time Square
Here or there.

All the same in the corporate church.

Selling sanctuary for less.

Air bags included.

Terminated.

"Fuck the algorithm!" the masses chanted.

Proof that Skynet had won.

construction

Be careful what you say to me.
I'm more delicate than I may seem.

Faulty scaffolding runs the lines of my thighs
and the curve of my cheek.

I have a structure to preserve
and these words you say are a demolition.

Blood, bone, and skin
line the ground, seal the wallpaper in.

And all you did was put up an ugly orange sign
to tell the new buyers
"watch your step."

2007

Cocktail Waitress

Cock Tail?

Cock Tale.

Well, there was that one time
[CELEBRITY NAME REDACTED
who was a supporting actor in Jerry Maguire]
slapped my ass hard
when I was working at a lounge in Santa Monica

and instead of being dumbfounded
and almost spilling my tray of martinis
I should have just handed him his fucking drink and said
"show me the money"
in his stupid Oscar-winning voice
instead of trying to get him kicked out of the bar

because none of those cocky celebrities ever got kicked out of the bar.

Not one of them.

Just one more?

What a mistake.
What an intoxicating mess.

Midnight.
Last Call.

The genie lured me into the bottle with her
and we cooked up a potion special just for you.

I hadn't counted on the recipe going all so horribly wrong.

Incorrect measurements.

Bubbling over the bottle's edge
staining the clean white tablecloths.

An apothecary lined with a dash of this and a scrape of that
with only the choice to drink.

Fine Dining Fight Club

This act is criminal,
the unprecise placement of the fork.

Back-waiters at the ready,
with water jugs secretly empty.

And servers no longer agreeing
with every request, VIPs seething.

A quiet crisp-pressed dressed coupe.

Until the owner walks in,
and with that quick split second,
all order returns
in this front-of-house lead
reeling rebellion.

Penny Lane

EXT. Afternoon.

Two women rummage through the sale bin at the latest local trendy thrift shop and one of them picks up a long suede fur-lined coat.

- Hey, look at this coat, this fucking coat. You know that moment in "Almost Famous" when Kate Hudson's character Penny Lane realizes that all of her hopes and dreams between her and Billy Crudup's character are a bunch of lies?

  When Patrick Fugit's character tells her that she was traded for a six pack of beer? And she says "what kind beer" – all gorgeous and innocent with this amazing pain and inner strength in her eyes?

- Yah.

- That character. That fucking character. I always wanted a jacket like this. I always wanted to be her.

  Oh. It's on sale. Shit, it's only a dollar today.

- Well, for a limited time only, you can be her for only a hundred pennies.

- Fuck that. She ruined my twenties. I thought it was sexy to be used and ruined and broken.

But, she deserves to be worth more than a six pack of beer or a hundred pennies.

- Don't we all.
- Truth. I blame Cameron Crowe for all of my existential angst.
- Well, if you don't buy the coat, I will. It's classic.
- Oh, I'm definitely gonna buy it. You know, out of protest against misogyny. And then wear it as an ironic piece of feminist fashion.
- I support that choice. And now I want a beer.
- Yah, me too. Happy hour?
- For sure. We'll toast to Penny Lane.

  She should get her own movie really. I mean, she is the original "Band-Aid" after all.
- Agreed. I wonder if anyone has pitched that story?
- You should write it.
- Yes, damn it I should! Fuck, this coat is magic. Penny Lane has pulled me in once again.

the housewife in apartment 12B

one
two
three
four

she knocks down the basement door
tears floating on the floor
of this bloodied silent house.

fairy tales and handmaid's wails
singing from the cupboard they sail
from behind the salt and pepper veil
used to feed your laughter.

it's all in the way your fingers pry
into each hidden space they spy
so her bones are sucked all the meat now dry
in your ringed fingered clutches.

and like a servant she tends to you
giving you each fantasy brand new
and all you do is sit and stew
then muzzle her ever after.

2013

The Assassination

This is messy.

The snake inside of me
twists violently
while the devil clutches
my aching tongue.

Lost and churning
aching and burning
for a release that
never comes.

I stepped into this willingly.

In front of this firing squad
sniper lined with the
dirty windowpane
ready to open fire.

I don't even hear it.
Don't even feel it.

My heart splattered
on the freshly painted bedroom wall.

A Rorschach.

the expedition

It's volatile and dangerous in there.

Jim Morrison said
"the cunt grips him like a warm friendly hand"
but I have to warn you
tell you
there is caution tape over this land

volcanoes and tornadoes meet here
souls breed and die here
Fiona Apple screams and cries here

and if I had you near
you would implode
ashes to ashes
dust to dust

but still

you want to go on an expedition
searching through me for my heart
the heart that will tear you apart
and devour you altogether.

For Cindy: My Blue Valentine

She falls into me like the return home
after a quivering astral projection
burrowing into my chest.

Her words on my tongue rolling over
lips that have never spoken before
in this small space between skin and soul.

I know her better than myself.
The way her heart aches
body pulses
for a strong touch
and the desperate desire to flee.

Both hope and sorrow
live inside
in the pre-tremble, in the in-between.

And I house her, hide her, conceal her.

Until our final swan song embeds her forever into me.

And yet
someone else will take her words
take her wants
and they

themselves
will become
her.
Home.

This Will Be Televised

We live for these moments between Action and Cut.
Heart's script open to divulge
all of its quietest dark secrets.

We dream for these moments between Action and Cut.
Backdropped stages all more real than
our current curbed reality.

We die for these moments between Action and Cut.
Guns and violence clenching
your aching, churning gut.

All only propelling fascination
without any real obligation
to the true humiliation
of humanity.

inside these moving pictures

sticky synthetic red carpet laid out before us
we strut along
smiling for their Q and A

an unveiling
a wailing
under the billboard of giant faces
and places
of people we have never been
and places we will never be

our premiere
of something
starring someone
from the latest news cycle of fame

Hollywood Blvd

hot biting charred asphalt underneath our feet
a glistening, black yellow brick road
to follow
toward a dark dank theater

and somewhere here
we are captured in a hypnotic fever

forever
like a perfectly produced negative
on film

Paul-y Pocket.

I want to put you away,
snug,
into my pocket.

I know you won't be happy there
nestled underneath the lint and hair
yet all I want is to keep you there
so that you can't leave me.

But I know you're being warned
and all my attempts are stillborn
and I can't keep you here enclosed with me.

So instead I let you go

and oh, my dear Pauly, oh

I'm left with a gaping threadbare hole

a hole here deep within me.

Social-ism

Absence of Influence
Apparently irrelevant
Completely insignificant
Nowhere near Brilliant
Wondering
Where
the
fuck
I
went
?

140 Characters

Is this a poem
or a tweet?
Is this a poem
or a tweet?
Is this a poem
or a tweet?
Is this a poem
or a tweet?
Is this a poem
or a tweet?
Is this a poem
or a tweet?
Is this a poem
or a tweet?

2016

Road Trip Renegade

My whisper echoes in the mountain valley
toward the setting sun.

It begs for bars and handcuffs
and a smooth key to stifle
my loaded glove compartment gun.

But finger on the trigger
it lingers
and instead of prison
it's a submission
and we are off on a journey
across America.
across the Universe.

Pulling
taunting
trivial travel.

Lost in a road map
of
too many lefts
too many exists
too many ways out.

No jail for the weary now
the wicked frown
the silver tongued
suspects
on trial for all of our silent sins.

And all I want to do is stop at a dusty desert roadside diner
for a bitter coffee and home fries
and America's true Americana served to me
for my last meal.

Captive.

Could I be your girl?
Your golden lioness?
These animalistic sounds I make
luring you in
like you are on a safari peering at me
through the warm glass window
of your drive-by bus tour.

You see me as delicate, for your roughened hands
to caress and to play with
contorting my tiny arms and legs.
Like a cheerful zookeeper
you brag that you are the maker
of the noose knotted name tag
and collar you place on my neck
bringing me home.

Sitting curled up beside you
I purr a soft song
through gritty bloodied fangs
singing you into a state of deep dark sleep
watching
from my wide-open cage
waiting for the moment
for the instant
to pounce.

Natural Selection

It's all topsy turvy
turning
sounds of the whooping crane
wailing crying birds of prey
no longer petrified to fly.

It's all in the evolution, in Darwin
natural selection
survival of the fittest no matter what the means.

And we are not fit.

Crammed into this tomb humankind shares
buried underneath the place where animals tread
all over us.
Worms burrow into our top later
calling us home.
We are their palace to eat in, breathe in, sleep in, die in.
as life leaves us and feeds into them.

Until it all flips upside down
to what we think is right-side up
north to south, south to north.
and back again.

And the earth evolves.

Eats us whole.

Cleansing the rot.

Reclaiming
what is rightly theirs.

Sadie and the Salton Sea

Jeff Buckley played
on the battered CD player of the old blue Ford truck.

A hazy red sun setting as her painted backdrop
hanging in the sky like she could have pulled it down from heaven
blanketing the road behind her
a thick canvas curtain
shielding her from the road before.

She stopped along the barren Salton Sea
in Bombay Beach
a non-town, hometown
so that she could set alight her dreams
by a burned-out beige couch down the street from the uninhabited RVs.

She lights a Marlboro cigarette
eyes softly closed, as hair loosely flows
and she snaps a photo
with her Canon camera and Bluetooth remote
perfectly curated for her Instagram feed.

This is the place where seekers go.

Where you can be everything and nothing.
Where the image you capture
can both damage and repair.
Where you are no one and everyone.
A stranger a lover a child a mother.
Your own lost and found
among the salty sea air
and the disrepair of all of the other
souls that have passed through this place in purgatory.

The circumference of time would await her.

Taking photos of herself along the way
from Salvation Mountain
to Slab City and The Range
circling west to the Salton Sea's strange Salton City.

And in that 116 mile journey
round the dead water
Sadie would find herself after sunset
breathing in and swimming in the desert's dark dry air
rounding the bend back up towards Highway 10 in that blue
Ford truck.

But now
with the perfect photos
to make
her ennui
beautiful

purposeful
and
influential.

Hopefully forever.

But probably
never.

2020

Writer's Block

Vignettes
Epithets
Pieces of a life.

Short scenes and fragmented dreams.

Highlighted cruelly by a blinking cursor.

Truth be told
I no longer wanted to hold
the catastrophe of
and
the creation of
a beginning, middle, and end.

So here is the file
sent to you in Final Draft
so you can create your own twisted mystery
sleuth your own enigmatic discovery
because I no longer want the responsibility
of this
tragic intellectual property.

Happily

She didn't want to be a mother.

They said there was a promise of what could be,
what would be,
what should be,
if she
would only see the meaning.

But it's a meandering
a shifting
a capturing
a re-telling
of a story that she
is not the speaker of.

They are her unreliable narrators
a fabled tertiary source.

It's a fairy-tale told in silence.

Eyes upon eyes upon eyes
with everyone holding their breath
without blinking
without thinking
that maybe
she has the right to be the author of it all.

So here she begins on page one
of her "Once Upon"
and even though the voices aren't gone
she will no longer long
for anyone's editorial approval
any "advanced reader copy" opinions
or their criticism
on her Happily Ever, or Happily Never.

It's of no consequence to them
and she can finally condemn
the will
of other
women.

a long dark summer

The light that went up on the stage that night
captured a worried woman in a pandemic flight
just at the end of her opening monologue
before any dialogue
seizing meaning
in a scattered meandering
and a script with no ending
fending
for her life.

But the Director had no direction.

Like being given a road map to nowhere
when nowhere was <u>the</u> where to go.

But how would that Maestro know?

"A Long Dark Summer" would be taught later on
as the stage-play of reckoning
of overturning meaning
of purposely steaming
in the oppressive heat
of that unrelenting spotlight sun.

And as she stood there,
her OCD became a personal sunk cost fallacy.

And she would propose
the play's new purpose
to fall into the chaotic serene abyss
of this crowded darkened theater.

Synesthesia
through scripted media
with everyone in the audience waiting
for the curtain call
of a never-ending credit roll
and the collective applause for a heightened cause
of the many I-s and You-s and We-s.

punctuate

; however, this is where my story begins
in the middle of the page
in the height of the semicolon
in all of the what ifs and buts and could bes
meet me at the end
and we'll see
if the period's placement
is all that it should be
or if commas
are all the more
necessary.

2021

All the world's a stage.

She looked out to the audience.
Looked out to the audience
Looked out to
Looked out
Looked
Look

Acknowledgements

Thank you to my incredible husband Barry W. Levy. You make every single day an adventure and an absolute joy.

To my Mom and Dad, Bobbie Muralt and Ruben Santos, thank you for always supporting me and believing in me and my creative heart.

Granny, I miss you every day. Thank you for your strength, love, and security.

To my dear friends and family, I am so endlessly grateful for each and every one of you, whether we talk every day or every few years. You all make up the tapestry of my world, and each conversation and experience fuels me. I thrive on the connection we all have in the big and small ways.

To the community of artists who surround me in person and online, thank you for all of your bravery. We are powerful, magical, and our voices matter. Thank you for every single piece of art that you create.

About the Author

Helenna Santos is an actor, writer, and producer with *Mighty Pharaoh Films*. She was the founder/editor-in-chief of the entertainment website *Ms. In The Biz* for its seven year run.

She has appeared in many network TV shows as well as feature films and national commercials. She also voices animated characters and narrates audiobooks and commercial campaigns.

Her work as a contributing writer has been featured in a variety of publications including *MovieMaker, Backstage, WeScreenplay,* and *BUST* Magazine.

Helenna is a mix of Filipino/Russian/German heritage, a US and Canadian dual citizen, and currently resides in Vancouver, BC with her husband and their Bernedoodle pup.

Site: helennasantos.com
Twitter: @helennamsantos
Instagram: @helennamsantos

www.ingramcontent.com/pod-product-compliance
Lightning Source LLC
LaVergne TN
LVHW041548070426
835507LV00011B/987